*The need of a college, Catholic in spirit and under
Catholic auspices, is most evident, considering especially
the steady growth in the number of inhabitants of the
Diocese during the last twenty years.
Convinced of the expediency of such a college, and having
with continued interest followed throughout the last forty
years the work of the Dominican Fathers in New England,
I hereby extend an invitation to said religious community
of the Province of St. Joseph... to found within the limits of
the Diocese of Providence, a college....*

Bishop Matthew Harkins, from a letter to the Fathers of the
Province of St. Joseph, October 9, 1915.

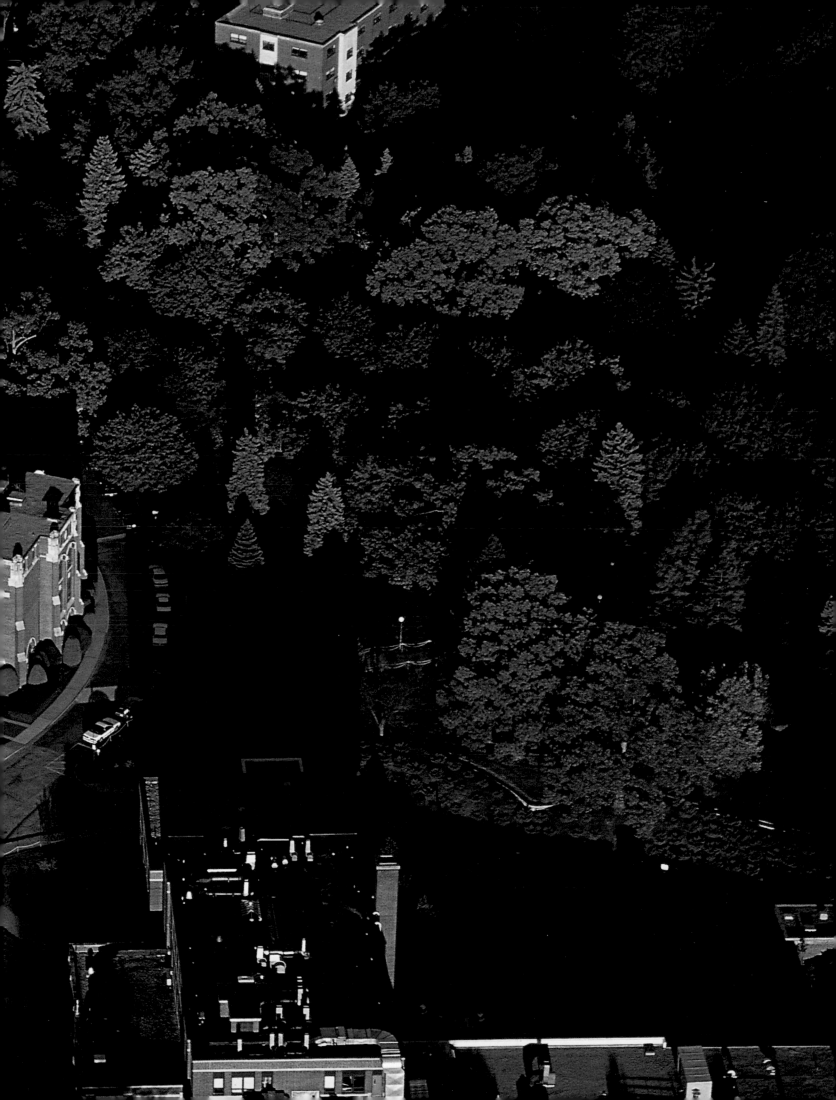

HARKINS
HALL

THEN AND NOW
PROVIDENCE COLLEGE

Photographed by Brian Smith

Harmony House

Publishers Louisville

Sincere thanks to the Providence College community for its assistance during the production of this book, and especially to the following: James F. Quigley, O.P., Executive Vice President; R.B. Haller, O.P., Assistant VP for Institutional Relations/Director of College Events; Ann Manchester-Molak, Executive Director, Office of Public Relations; Joseph Tortorici, O.P., Executive Director, Residence Life Office; Michael A. Haveles, Executive Director, Food Services Department; Diane Childs Comerford, Director of Alumni Relations; G. Adrian Dabash, O.P., Chaplain; Jane M. Jackson, Director of Archives; Mary Christine Sullivan, Archival Assistant; Mark Rapoza, Assistant to the Director for Operations, Residence Life Office; Ann L. Iannotti, Principal Secretary, Office of Public Relations; and the Physical Plant Department.

Executive Editors: William Butler and William Strode
Library of Congress Catalog Number: 91-70927
Hardcover International Standard Book Number 0-916509-89-3
Printed in the Republic of Korea by Sung In Printing Company, LTD.
through Vivid Color Separation, New York, N.Y.
First Edition printed Spring 1992 by Harmony House Publishers,
P.O. Box 90, Prospect, Kentucky 40059 (502) 228-2010 / 228-4446
Copyright © 1992 by Harmony House Publishers
Photographs copyright © 1992 by Brian Smith

INTRODUCTION

By Dr. Donna T. McCaffrey
Assistant Professor of History

"In all the world, there is nothing so curious and interesting and so beautiful as truth."
Agatha Christie

Anno Domini 1992 marks the celebration of Providence College's seventy-fifth anniversary. This visual journey, held in hand, flicks into permanency photographic moments and memories, edifices of stone, acmes of glory, human achievement, and warm familial recollections. This work is an invitation to recall, rejoin, and reflect upon Providence College.

To begin that reflection, perhaps it is appropriate to ask: What is Providence College? Is Providence College the "Mother of Truth," hailed as such by three generations in the opening phrase of the Alma Mater? Is Providence College "Veritas," truth itself, as the motto proclaims? Or is Providence College these and still more — a unique, enduring, organic community dedicated to excellence in higher education and the pursuit of truth? As in all great human mystery, the answer lies in the origins, evolution, and actualization of the entity; or as Cicero proclaims, "The worth of human life . . . is woven into the life of our ancestors by the records of history." Thus, what Providence College is, will be found in its history, a history of people: people with an idea, people who believed in God, people with courage, and people willing to sacrifice self to realize an educational ideal irrevocably fixed in the photographic record of time and space which follows.

In a sense, the history of Providence College began more than 775 years ago. Dominic Guzman, a Spanish nobleman, embraced poverty and had an idea. He wanted to establish an order "for preaching and the salvation of souls." He petitioned the papacy and, on December 22, 1216, Pope Honorius III gave his support to Dominic's idea and declared the Order of Preachers "inviolable for all time to come." In his Bull of 1216, Pope Honorius prophesied that Dominic's brethren would be "champions of the faith and true lights of the world."

Dominic immediately sent his sons to study at the great European universities. Where they went to study, they remained to teach. St. Thomas Aquinas took Dominic's idea and affirmed that teaching was one of the essential objects of the Order and in his Apologia for Religious Orders argued the appropriateness of the teaching apostolate for religious. For the next six centuries the Dominicans held the teaching chairs of Scripture and Theology at nearly all the major European universities — from Oxford to Lyons, Paris, Bologna, Bordeaux, Cologne, Milan, and Valencia. By the nineteenth century a host of Dominican men and women had carried on the Dominican teaching tradition throughout Europe. The idea then crossed the Atlantic Ocean.

In Europe at the time of the persecution of Catholics in England and the Napoleonic Purges on the continent, American-born Dominican Father Edward Dominic Fenwick had an idea — to bring the Dominican Order to the newly formed United States. Fenwick wanted to begin his American foundation with a college. He came home in November 1804 ready to found a college in Maryland on the property his family owned. Yet, first, U.S. Bishop John Carroll was in desperate need of missionaries for the dangerous wild frontier of Kentucky. Sacrificing his collegiate idea to the pressing needs of the infant U.S., Fenwick and his small band of three traveled west, by foot or on horseback, to bring the faith to the pioneers. For the next sixty years the persistent theme of the Dominican college apostolate was a dominant influence in Fenwick's Province of Saint Joseph. Before the Civil War, three Dominican colleges were opened in Kentucky, Ohio, and Wisconsin. Alumni included three U.S. bishops, scores of future missionary priests, and Jefferson Davis. The Fenwick ideal of a Dominican teaching apostolate was strongly entrenched in the American Order of Preachers. They were ready to respond to the call of the Bishop of Providence, Rhode Island.

Irish Bostonian Matthew Harkins went, as a young priest in 1884, to the Third Plenary Council of Baltimore. The American Catholic Church was in crisis, faced with an overwhelming influx of Catholic immigrants, beset by a vicious nativist anti-Catholic movement, and persecuted by strong prejudice ingrained in a predominantly Protestant country. Harkins listened at the Council of Bishops to the plea of Bishop John Lancaster Spalding:

We live in the midst of millions who still bear the yoke of inherited prejudices and who, because for three hundred years real cultivation of mind was denied to Catholics who spoke English, conclude that Protestantism is the source of enlightenment and the Church the Mother of ignorance.

Young Harkins caught the fire and passion of Spaulding's appeal:

To be intellectually the equals of others, we Catholics must have with them equal advantage of education, and so long as we look rather to the multiplying of schools and seminaries than to the creation of a real university our progress will be slow and uncertain, because a university is the great ordinary means to the best cultivation of the mind.

Within three years Matthew Harkins was named Bishop of Providence and began immediately the construction of a Catholic education system in his diocese. He dreamed of a capstone to this edifice — a Catholic college.

By 1915 Harkins found a man equally strong in devotion to Catholic education. Father Raymond Meagher, Irish Bostonian Provincial of the Dominican Province of Saint Joseph, was committed to the Dominican seven-hundred-year-old tradition and to Fenwick's American dream. Harkins and Meagher joined forces to make the idea a reality. With courage and boldness bordering on the foolhardy, they trusted in God to take care of the specifics, while they rolled up their sleeves and did everything but dig the foundation for Harkins Hall. Bishop Harkins scraped funds together to buy eleven acres of land for the college site. Meagher set about getting permission for the foundation from the Dominican Master General in Rome and applying to the papacy for permission. He wrote Pope Benedict XV for permission to found a house "to educate in piety and letters the youth of the city of Providence." On January 18, 1917, the Bishop arranged for a bill to be introduced in the Rhode Island legislature and, by February 14, 1917, An Act to Incorporate Providence College was passed. The papal consent was stalled when the documents from Rome were sunk by a German torpedo in World War I; but written papal consent was secured by February 28, 1917. Harkins bought seven more acres and, when the first Providence College Corporation meeting was held, the college received a land grant of eighteen acres from the Bishop and $10,000. Father Meagher pledged the Dominican teachers and $25,000 to start the first building. Harkins brought his ideas to his people. A wave of enthusiasm over the prospect of a Catholic college swept the state of Rhode Island. Many wealthy Catholics contributed to Harkins' fund-raising program to raise $200,000, but the bulk of the donations came from those of modest means — the poor classes of laboring Catholic immigrants giving beyond what they could afford. Added to the major fund-raising efforts were a host of other events, such as rummage sales and bake sales of Irish soda bread and Italian cannoli. By May 23, 1918, $156,139.73 was raised, and ground was broken for the first building — Harkins Hall (Bishop Harkins would not allow the college to be named after himself). World War I held up the opening for a full year. Then on May 22, 1919, the dedication of the new college coincided with Bishop Harkins' fiftieth anniversary of ordination. On September 17, 1919, with seventy-one students and nine Dominican faculty, Providence College opened her doors, pledged to a particular educational system. This pedagogy was basically "the scholastic system, adapted from Aristotle and the Ancient Greeks, Christianized by Thomas Aquinas and Albertus Magnus, and successfully carried out by the Order of Preachers for seven centuries in the great universities."

In the line of Dominic, Fenwick, Harkins, and Meagher, for the next seventy-five years Providence College grew and prospered. Early Presidents Albert D. Casey, O.P. (1919-1921); William D. Noon, O.P. (1921-1927); Lorenzo C. McCarthy, O.P. (1927-1936); John J. Dillon, O.P. (1936-1944); and Frederick C. Foley, O.P. (1945-1947) guided Providence College through her youthful, struggling early history. Providence College overcame the obstacles raised by World War I, and survived the Great Depression and plummeting enrollment caused by World War II. Providence College grew from eighteen to forty-five and a half acres, from one building to seven, and produced approximately 2,500 alumni by 1947.

From nine Dominicans in 1919 to eighty-six laboring by 1947 and from one layman in 1929 to approximately eighteen laymen in 1947, the faculty ranks swelled to implement a curriculum leading to degrees of Bachelor of Arts, Bachelor of Philosophy, Bachelor of Science, or a two-year Pre-Medical Certificate meeting the then-requirements of the American Medical Association.

Fundamental to all five presidencies was the Catholic identity of the college, the retention of the seven-hundred-year-old scholastic nucleus, a strong commitment to liberal arts, and a successful adaptation to the trends of higher education set by regional and national accrediting associations. The idea of the founders, a Catholic college in Rhode Island, came of age.

From the solid foundations laid in the first thirty years, Providence College matured into a modern, fully accredited Catholic liberal arts college under the next five presidencies of Robert J. Slavin, O.P. (1947-1961); Vincent C. Dore, O.P. (1961-1965); William P. Haas, O.P. (1965-1971); Thomas R. Peterson, O.P. (1971-1985); and John F. Cunningham, O.P. (1985 to the present).

These later Dominican presidents, committed to the idea of the founders and early fathers, have carried the college forward through adversity, economic crisis, national decrease in all-male college enrollments, the Korean War, the Vietnam War, oil embargoes, the civil rights and students' rights movements of the sixties, admission of women in 1971, the tragic death of ten women in the Aquinas dormitory fire of 1977, the blizzard of 1978, and the Persian Gulf War.

The labors of these presidents culminated in national academic recognition for PC. In 1991 Providence College was ranked by *The National Review* among America's fifty top liberal arts colleges, and in 1990 by Barron's as one of the three hundred best buys in the United States. Additionally, *U.S. News & World Report* in both 1990 and 1991 listed Providence College sixth in the North Regional Category of colleges.

In the past forty-five years, the Providence College campus grew to approximately 105 acres with the addition of the adjacent Sisters of Good Shepherd and the Chapin Hospital properties. Through the arduous procurement of funds from loyal alumni, capital fund campaigns, loans, grants, and the continued contributed service of Dominican administrators and faculty, the expansion of the campus mission to higher education was achieved.

By 1992 Providence College grew to over fifty-four facilities, including administration and classroom buildings, a science complex, an award-winning library with approximately 300,000 holdings, art and music buildings, Dominican residence, fourteen student residences, three athletic buildings with pool, ice rink, and indoor courts and track, three indoor and one outdoor chapel, a student recreation center, two cafeterias, and eleven parking areas. This impressive physical plant is self-contained in a park-like setting located in the midst of a thriving New England city.

In 1991 the 287 teaching faculty members consisted of 217 full-time and seventy visiting and adjunct professors, including forty Dominican Fathers and eight Dominican Sisters. Over 73 percent hold doctorates. Thirty-seven academic majors and programs for approximately 3,800 undergraduate students lead to the Bachelor of Arts and Bachelor of Science degrees.

Providence College's School of Continuing Education, which has been providing adult learners with a quality undergraduate educational experience in the liberal arts as well as business and professional disciplines, serves as a vital link to the community.

The scholarly milieu and academic community is enhanced by a growing Graduate School. Proposed in 1963 and nurtured and guided by Cornelius P. Forster, O.P., the Graduate School enrolls approximately six hundred students yearly. Since 1964, over 3,471 students have been awarded an M.A., M.S., M.Ed., M.B.A., or Ph.D. from the Graduate School of Providence College.

Poised on the threshold of the third millenium, more than 28,000 alumni bear the impress of Providence College as an indelible mark on their character and service in society.

People with an idea, with courage, with a belief in God, and the pursuit of truth have sacrificed to realize this educational ideal. As Senator John O. Pastore remarked to then-Vice President Walter Mondale in 1978, "Providence College has wrought a social and intellectual revolution in the State of Rhode Island" — and, as we have seen, from this state unto the nation.

Agatha Christie wrote that "in all the world, there is nothing so curious and so interesting and so beautiful as truth." What an apt description of Providence College. Enjoy this visual seventy-five year journey through Providence College — a community committed and dedicated to the pursuit of truth and excellence in Catholic higher education.

The War Memorial Grotto

Aquinas Hall

Dominic Hall

This college has labored in love, the sacrificing service of minds to mold other minds, hearts to inspire other hearts....

Former Senator John O. Pastore, from his address at the Capital Program Dinner, 1969

Aquinas Hall Lounge

Be neither intimidated nor intransigent; and never settle for a nice warm feeling; be smart in heeding the wisdom of others, be courageous in thinking for yourself, be honest in all that you say and do.

John C. Quinn, '45, Commencement Address, 1985

Blackfriars Theatre

Hunt-Cavanagh Hall

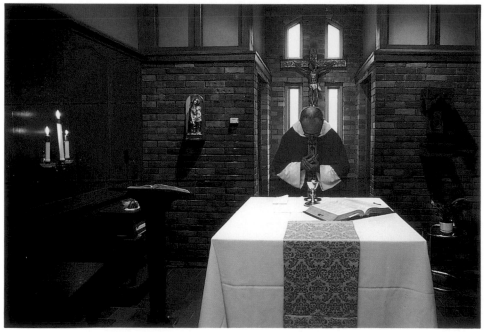

Harkins Hall, student oratory

Hendricken Field

Alumni Hall Gymnasium

Peterson Recreation Center

Providence Civic Center

Commencement Ball

Apartment Complex

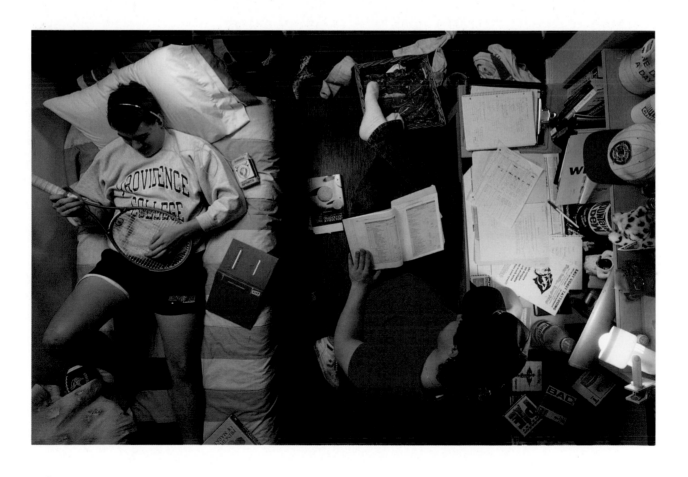

Harvestfest

Reunion Weekend

St. Thomas Aquinas Priory/Gragnani Dominican Center

A ship in port is safe. That is not what ships are built for. And I want every one of you to be good ships and sail out into the future and do the things which we need done in the future for the future of this country.

Commodore Grace Murray Hopper, Commencement Address, 1984

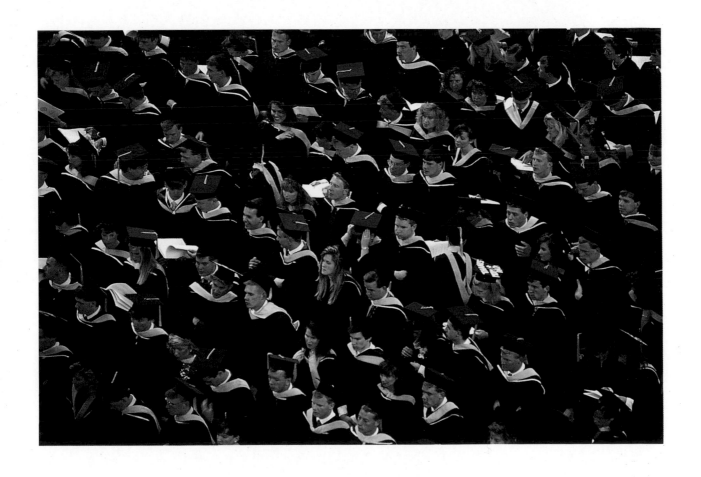

Providence College

A look at the past in photographs
from the College Archives

The President's House (Dominic Hall/Bailey House) 1950's

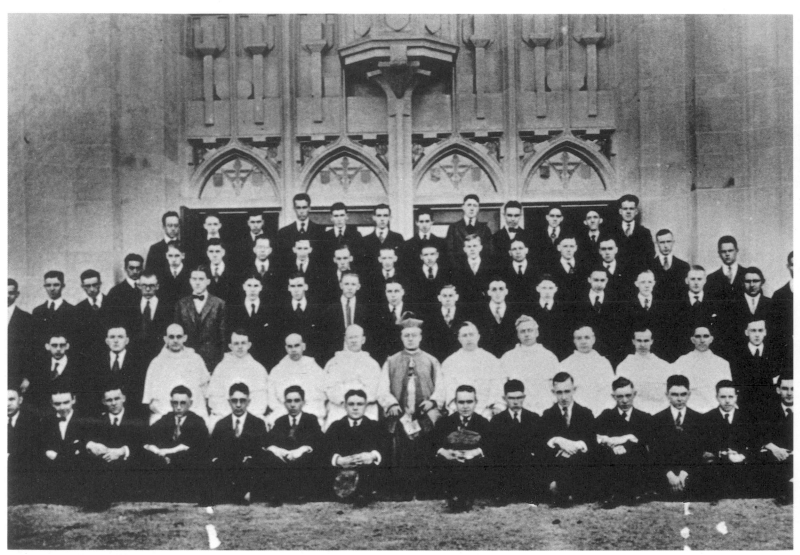

Faculty and First Class on Opening Day, September 18, 1919

Bishop Harkins Hall Dedication, May 25, 1919

The Second Commencement Ceremony, June 12, 1924

*Pyramid Players performing
"Hamlet," May 13, 1927*

Aerial view, pre-1927

Harkins Hall Addition construction, September 16, 1928

The Friars Club June 3, 1928

1928 Eastern College Baseball Champions

Providence College Football Team, 1927-1928

Judy Garland contributes to the Aquinas Hall Building Fund, February 19, 1938

Aquinas Hall construction, ca. 1939

Glenn Miller performs at the Class of 1940 Junior Promenade, May 8, 1939

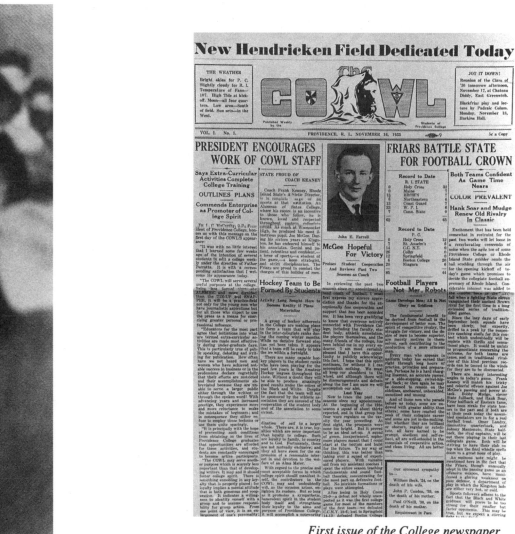

First issue of the College newspaper

War Memorial Grotto Dedication, May 9, 1948

Old Guzman Hall (Martin Hall/Bradley House), 1940's

The cast of "Who's Who," performed by the pre-ecclesiastical students of The Philomosian Players, February 22-24, 1922

Basketball in Harkins Hall Gymnasium, Lowell Textile Institute versus P.C., January 30, 1943

The 563 soldiers in Army Specialized Training Program Unit 1188 march off campus, March 19, 1944

Opening of the Gymnasium Fund Drive, January 25, 1944

A HISTORY OF PROVIDENCE COLLEGE

1216 Pope Honorius III grants permission to St. Dominic Guzman to found the Order of Preachers.

1274 Death of St. Thomas Aquinas, patron Saint of Catholic schools and preeminent Dominican philosopher and theologian.

1910 The Provincial Council accepts a petition from Bishop Matthew Harkins, D.D., to establish a college in Providence but requests time to provide adequate staffing.

1915 Bishop Harkins writes to the Provincial, James Raymond Meagher, O.P., extending the formal invitation to the Dominican Fathers of the Province of St. Joseph to found a college.

1916 Provincial James Raymond Meagher, O.P., relays the Master General's approval to Bishop Harkins; Provincial designates Dennis Albert Casey, O.P., as the person to oversee establishment of the college.

1917 Governor signs the bill incorporating Providence College; Master General receives the blessing of Pope Benedict XV for the "establishment of a House in the City of Providence to educate youth in religion and letters"; Bishop Harkins grants the Dominican Fathers of the Province of St. Joseph the tract of land on which to build the college.

1918 Corporation election of Dennis Albert Casey, O.P., as the first president; Due to WWI, the Corporation postpones the scheduled opening; Harkins Hall Chapel is the site of the first St. Pius Parish mass.

1919 Bishop Harkins Hall dedication; Providence College opening ceremonies; Providence College Orchestra, the oldest organization open to the general student population, debuts.

1920 Providence College students hold their first social event, a whist and promenade, at the Narragansett Hotel; College's first theatrical production, "A Thief in the House"; Providence College plays in its first intercollegiate athletic contest, an exhibition basketball game against Rhode Island State College, losing 87-25; The first issue of the *Alembic*, the oldest student publication.

1921 Closing day exercises include awarding of the first pre-medical certificates; College confers its first degree, an Honorary Doctor of Laws, on Italian WWI General Armando Diaz.

1922 Over 3,000 attend the opening football game on Hendricken Field (U.S. Submarine Base 42, P.C. 13).

1923 First Commencement; Formation of the Providence College Alumni Association.

1924 Providence College athletes gain national attention by playing in and eventually winning the longest (4 hrs. 17 min.) scoreless intercollegiate baseball game (P.C. 1, Brown University 0).

1926 College purchases the Bradley Estate; The college's first alumnae, 2 Dominican and 9 Mercy Sisters, include several of the pioneering students of 1918; After extensive renovations and construction of a three-story addition, Bradley House opens as Guzman Hall, a residence for Dominican pre-ecclesiastical students.

1927 Providence College confers its first Master of Arts degree on Daniel J. O'Neill.

1928 Largely through the efforts of John E. Farrell, the charter members of the Friars Club, the college's social representative, hold their organizational meeting.

1929 Harkins Hall addition dedication ceremony; St. Pius Parish moves off-campus, celebrating Easter Mass in its new church on Elmhurst Avenue; Announcement of the formation of Providence College Club of New York, the first alumni territorial group.

1931 Graduation of first layperson from the extension school.

1935 Inaugural issue of *The Cowl*.

1936 Revised extension school program includes night courses.

1939 Aquinas Hall opening.

1941 President approves the establishment of Veridames, "Ladies of Truth"; last Providence College varsity football game (Xavier University 33, P.C. 0).

1942 Due to WWII, Providence College inaugurates a year-round schedule.

1944 500-plus man Army Specialized Training

Program Unit marches off campus.

1947 Carolan Club formals expand into dorm weekends; Science Building (Albertus Magnus Hall) groundbreaking ceremony.

1948 War Memorial Grotto dedication; Students vote to accept the proposed Providence College Student Congress Constitution.

1951 Activation of Reserve Officers' Training Corps Transportation Unit Training Program.

1952 Class of 1952 votes to combine its gift with that of the Class of 1951 for construction of the Gateway Pillars.

1955 College purchases the House of Good Shepherd property; Gymnasium dedication as Alumni Hall.

1956 Gordie Holmes makes a dramatic shot at the buzzer, bringing Providence College upset win over the University of Notre Dame, 85-83.

1957 Pilot group of freshmen in the Arts Honors Program begins classes.

1959 Raymond Hall opening.

1960 College confers its first Veritas Medal on Congressman John E. Fogarty.

1961 Providence College wins its first National Invitation Tournament (P.C. 62, St. Louis University 59).

1962 Closing of the former Guzman Hall (later renamed Martin Hall) as a dormitory for Dominican students.

1964 Providence College loses in its first National Collegiate Athletic Association Hockey Final Four appearance (University of Michigan 3, P.C. 2); Newly formed Graduate School adds history courses to graduate level offerings in education, religious education and guidance, and the sciences.

1965 For the first time, a layperson assumes a Providence College Vice Presidency.

1966 American Association of University Professors recognizes the establishment of a Providence College chapter.

1967 Beginning of the last student mandatory retreat; Appointment of the first female to the full-time undergraduate faculty.

1968 First Faculty Senate meeting; Harkins Hall Library closes and the move into the new Phillips Memorial Library begins.

1969 College Union groundbreaking ceremony; President announces abolition of the dress code.

1970 Administration announces that the college will remain open during the Vietnam student strike, with attendance being a matter of conscience.

1971 Beginning of the first summer freshman orientation program; Pioneering coeds move into Aquinas Hall; Introduction of interdisciplinary Development of Western Civilzation Program; President signs the Student Bill of Rights.

1972 First official Providence College game in the Providence Civic Center (P.C. 93, Fairfield University 57).

1973 Lady Friars play their first intercollegiate basketball game (P.C. 44, Southeastern Massachusetts University 41); P.C. loses in its first National Collegiate Athletic Association Basketball Final Four appearance (Memphis State University 98, P.C. 85).

1974 Providence College Cross Country Team wins the first of eleven consecutive New England championships; College purchases the Charles V. Chapin Hospital property.

1975 Graduation of the first co-educational class.

1976 Fine Arts Center opening exhibition.

1977 Aquinas Hall fire, which takes the lives of 10 students.

1978 Admissions Director reports that for the first time women outnumber men in the freshman class.

1979 Beginning of the academic year in which for the first time the majority of freshmen are from outside Rhode Island.

1981 Dedication of fieldhouse as Peterson Recreation Center.

1984 St. Thomas Aquinas Priory-Gragnani Dominican Faculty Residence and Community Center open house.

1988 Opening of three apartment-style residence halls.

College Entrance, 1947

A Formal Dance opens the First Carolan Club Dorm Weekend, February 14, 1947

The Faculty, 1936-1937

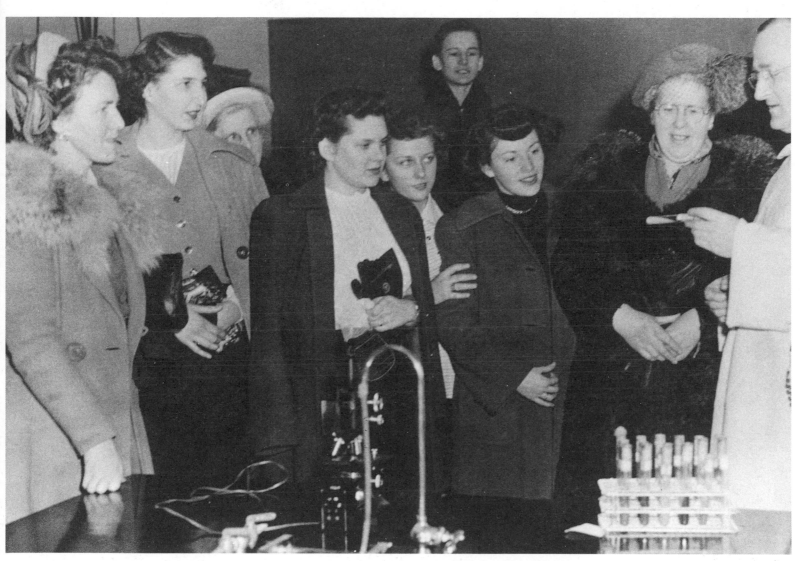

Faculty members conduct tours for the general public during the Dedication of Albertus Magnus Hall, January 29, 1949

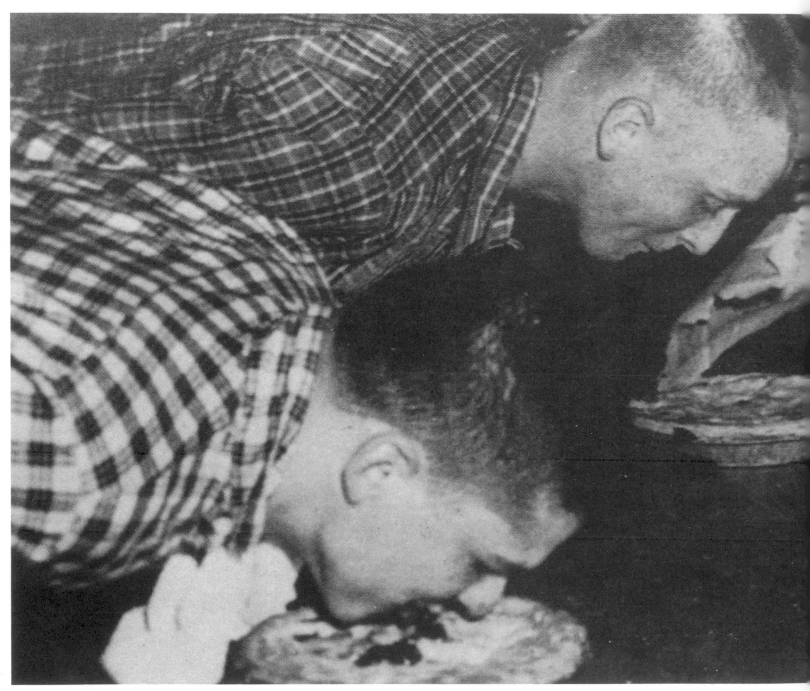

Farmer's Festival, November 16, 1956

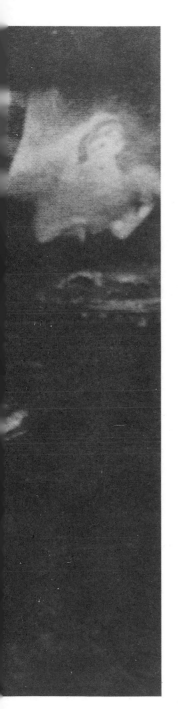

Alumni Ball at the 1st Homecoming Weekend, November 28, 1953

Study at Donnelly Hall, ca. 1949

Aquinas Hall Dining Room, ca. 1952

Varsity Track Team, 1949-1950

Aquinas Hall Chapel, 1962

The Military Ball, February 13, 1953

Harkins Hall Physics Lab, 1939

Reserve Officers' Training Corps Transportation Unit, 1952

Gordy Holmes' shot at the buzzer brings P.C. the upset win over the University of Notre Dame, February 14, 1956

Varsity Hockey returns, 1951-1952

Harkins Hall Library, 1950's

After missing this foul shot at the end of regulation time, Vinnie Ernst goes on to be the hero in the National Invitational Tournament semi-final win versus the College of the Holy Cross, March 23, 1961

The new Graduate School adds history courses to the College's Masters level offerings, 1964

The 50th Anniversary Academic Convocation includes groundbreaking for the College Union, September 27, 1969

Harkins Hall Bookstore during Freshman Orientation, 1958

Pioneering coeds move into Aquinas Hall, September 7, 1971

Students respond to administration rulings, February 6, 1969

Vietnam War Moratorium Day, October 15, 1969

Marvin Barnes and Kevin Stacom in the National Collegiate Athletic Association Final Four loss to Memphis State University, March 24, 1973